THE STORY OF THE
WASHINGTON

CREATIVE EDUCATION

Published by Creative Education
123 South Broad Street
Mankato, Minnesota 56001
Creative Education is an imprint of The Creative Company.

DESIGN AND PRODUCTION BY EVANSDAY DESIGN

PHOTOGRAPHS BY Getty Images (Bill Baptist / NBAE, Marie-Louise
Brimberg / National Geographic, Chris Hampson / NBAE, Focus on
Sport, Robert Lewis / NBAE, Francis Miller / Time & Life Pictures,
NBA Photo Library / NBAE, Doug Pensinger / Allsport, Richard
Piling / NBAE, Dale Tait / NBAE, Jerry Wachter / NBAE)

LIBRARY OF CONGRESS CATALOGING-IN-PUBLICATION DATA

Frisch, Aaron.
The story of the Washington Wizards / by Aaron Frisch.
p. cm. — (The NBA—a history of hoops)
Includes index.
ISBN-13: 978-1-58341-428-6
1. Washington Wizards (Basketball team)—History—
Juvenile literature. [1. Basketball—History—Juvenile literature.] I. Title. II. Series.

GV885.52.W37F75 2006
796.323'6409753—dc22   2006003978

First edition

9 8 7 6 5 4 3 2 1

COVER PHOTO: *Gilbert Arenas*

THE STORY OF THE
WASHINGTON
WIZARDS

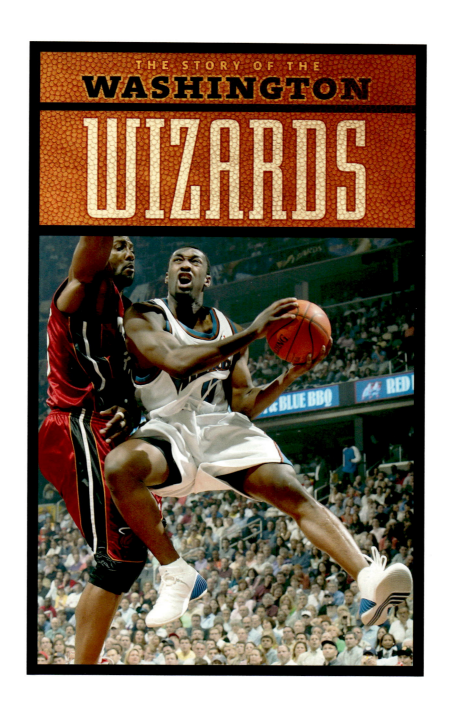

A A R O N   F R I S C H

C R E A T I V E   E D U C A T I O N

Kevin Loughery's quick hands

HARASSED THE OPPOSING GUARD INTO PUTTING UP A BAD SHOT. WES UNSELD, A BULL OF A CENTER, PULLED DOWN THE REBOUND, LOOKED UP THE COURT, AND RIFLED A PASS TO EARL MONROE. THE GUARD KNOWN AS "THE PEARL" QUICKLY DRIBBLED ACROSS HALF-COURT AND ZIPPED A LONG BOUNCE PASS TO GUS JOHNSON, WHO WAS SLASHING TO THE BASKET. JOHNSON CAUGHT THE PASS IN STRIDE AND LAID THE BALL SOFTLY OFF THE BACKBOARD AS THE ARENA ERUPTED IN NOISE. IT WAS WASHINGTON'S GLORY DAYS ON THE BASKETBALL COURT, AND THE BULLETS WERE FLYING.

WASHINGTON WIZARDS
Washington D.C.

1

WASHINGTON, D.C., THE CAPITAL OF THE UNITED States, occupies a section of government-owned land called the District of Columbia (D.C. for short) located between Maryland and Virginia. Many tourists travel to Washington to visit such famous buildings as the White House and such landmarks as the Washington Monument. Yet Washington is rich in more than just government history; it also has a long and storied sports tradition. One of those traditions involves a National Basketball Association (NBA) franchise named the Wizards, which settled in Washington in 1972.

The Wizards franchise was born in Chicago, Illinois, in 1961 as a team called the Packers (a name that changed to Zephyrs just a year later). The team had two terrific

9

WIZARDS

Home of the 555-foot Washington Monument, Washington, D.C., welcomed the NBA's Bullets in 1963

young players—center Walt Bellamy and sharpshooting forward Terry Dischinger—but it struggled for wins, and Chicagoans seemed uninterested. So, in 1963, the team's owners moved the franchise to Baltimore, Maryland, and renamed it the Bullets.

In 1964–65, the Bullets went just 37–43. But Bellamy and guard Don Ohl made headlines in the playoffs, leading the club all the way to the Western Division Finals. After that, the excitement died down until 1967, when the Bullets got a new coach and a new star. The coach was Gene Shue. The star was a 6-foot-3 guard named Earl "The Pearl" Monroe, selected with the second overall pick in the 1967 NBA Draft.

Even though Monroe had averaged more than 40 points per game in his final college season, some NBA scouts viewed his game as more style than substance. In his rookie season, Monroe put all doubts to rest by pouring in 24 points a game. His array of spin moves, tantalizingly high-bouncing dribble, and soaring, off-balance shots (which he called "flukey-duke" shots) left opponents shaking their heads. "That Monroe is unbelievable," said New York Knicks guard Walt Frazier after trying to stop the Bullets' young star. "I don't think The Pearl saw the basket on some of those shots."

"BELLS" Basketball seemed too easy for Walt Bellamy. The first draft pick of the new Chicago Packers in 1961, the agile center nicknamed "Bells" enjoyed one of the greatest rookie seasons in NBA history, averaging 31 points and 19 rebounds a game. He never matched those statistics again, but the 6-foot-10 Bellamy spent four terrific seasons with the Packers/Zephyrs/Bullets before starring for four other NBA teams. Bellamy was eventually enshrined in the Basketball Hall of Fame, but his talents never seemed to be fully appreciated during his time, as his laid-back personality was sometimes seen as laziness. "Walt wasn't a highly motivated player...," said Bob Leonard, who coached the Packers during Bellamy's rookie season. "He'd have some great games and then he'd have one where he didn't show up. But he was an excellent player."

WIZARDS

Famous showman Earl 'Monroe made up for a lack of speed with dazzling shooting and ball-handling skills

11

THE BULLETS FLY

MONROE COMBINED WITH FELLOW GUARD GUS JOHNSON to give Baltimore a strong scoring attack, but the team lacked a powerful post player and was often out-rebounded badly. In 1968, the Bullets cured that problem by spending their top pick in the NBA Draft on a 6-foot-7 center named Wes Unseld.

Unseld was the shortest center in the NBA, but he made up for it with his incredible strength; once he got into rebounding position, he was virtually impossible to move. In 1968–69, Unseld grabbed 18 boards per game, winning the NBA Most Valuable Player (MVP) award as a rookie. "Wes is just beautiful," said Bullets forward Ray Scott. "The other team shoots, Wes goes for the ball, and the rest of us go charging downcourt. He hits one of our guards at midcourt with one of those two-handed, over-the-head passes of his, and somebody else winds up with an easy layup."

13

WIZARDS

Strength, quickness, and sure hands made Wes Unseld a five-time All-Star and one-time NBA MVP

14

As durable as he was talented, Elvin Hayes missed only 9 games during his 16-season NBA career

With Unseld and Monroe leading the way, the Bullets emerged as one of the league's most powerful teams in the late 1960s and early '70s. They reached the NBA Finals in 1971, only to be swept by the Milwaukee Bucks and star center Lew Alcindor.

By 1973, the Bullets featured a revamped lineup. Monroe had been traded, forward Elvin Hayes added, and the club temporarily moved into a college arena while waiting for the new Capital Centre, on the outskirts of nearby Washington, to be completed. The "new" Bullets were an instant hit with fans. Besides Unseld, the biggest reason for their popularity was Hayes. Known as "The Big E," Hayes was a sensational all-around player who consistently averaged more than 20 points and 10 rebounds a game.

In the 1975 playoffs, Hayes and guard Phil Chenier helped the 60–22 Bullets charge back to the NBA Finals. Unfortunately, they again fell short of a championship. Although most experts expected Washington's loaded lineup to blow out the Golden State Warriors, the Warriors used exceptional teamwork to win the series in a stunning four-game sweep. As Warriors star Rick Barry summed up, "It has to be the greatest upset in the history of the NBA Finals."

52 EITHER WAY

It was no great surprise when the Bullets crushed the Portland Trail Blazers 156–104 in a November 1970 game, setting franchise records for most points scored in a game and largest margin of victory with the 52-point win. After all, the Bullets were one of the league's highest-scoring teams and featured Hall-of-Famers Wes Unseld and Earl "The Pearl" Monroe, while the Trail Blazers were an expansion team. It was shocking, however, when the Bullets set a team record for largest margin of defeat just six weeks later, this time losing by… 52 points. That 151–99 loss to the Milwaukee Bucks in January 1971 meant that the Bullets had swung 104 points in the wrong direction in just 21 games. By 2006, both of these "margin" records remained intact.

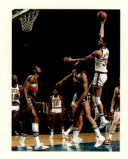

Three seasons later, though, Washington was back. The Bullets had a new coach named Dick Motta. They also had the best collection of big men in the NBA: Unseld, Hayes, and Bob Dandridge, a quick-scoring forward. This lineup went a mere 44–38 in 1977–78 but hit its stride in the playoffs, toppling three playoff opponents to reach the NBA Finals for the third time in franchise history. Washington's opponent this time was the Seattle SuperSonics. The Bullets were now the underdogs, but they had learned some lessons in the value of teamwork.

After six games, the series stood tied. In the deciding Game 7 in front of a raucous Seattle crowd, the SuperSonics worked furiously to overcome a slim Bullets' lead late in the fourth quarter. But Washington was not about to let another championship slip away. Unseld grabbed two critical rebounds in the final minute and sank two late free throws to preserve a 105–99 victory and send Washington fans into a frenzy of celebration. "What made the championship so great," said Coach Motta, "was that we weren't supposed to win it."

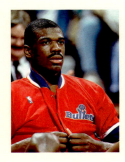

COMEBACK KING

Known for his lightning-quick jump shot, Bernard King was one of the NBA's brightest stars in the mid-1980s. In 1984–85, the New York Knicks forward led the league in scoring with almost 33 points a game. Near the end of that season, however, he tore a ligament in his right knee. The injury was so devastating that he missed almost two whole seasons, and the Knicks cut him. But King refused to give up. Given a chance with the Bullets in 1987, he gradually re-developed his skills. In 1990–91, he capped his miraculous comeback by netting 28 points per game and earning a place on the NBA All-Star team. "To come back after the entire knee was reconstructed," King said, "... [is] something that I'm awfully proud of."

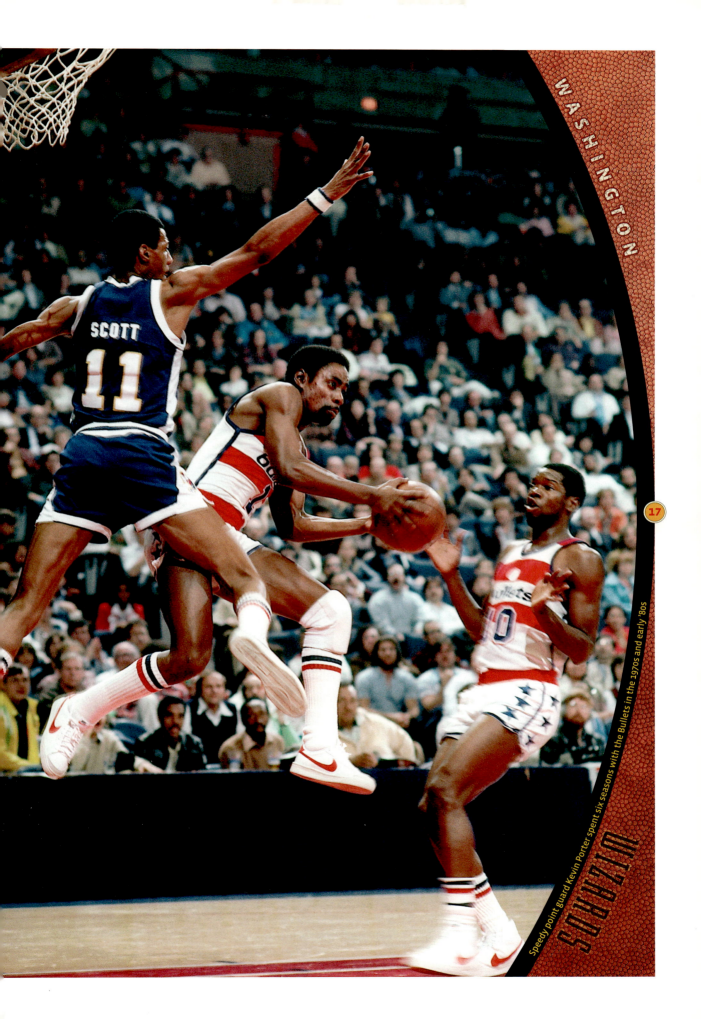

WIZARDS

Speedy point guard Kevin Porter spent six seasons with the Bullets in the 1970s and early '80s

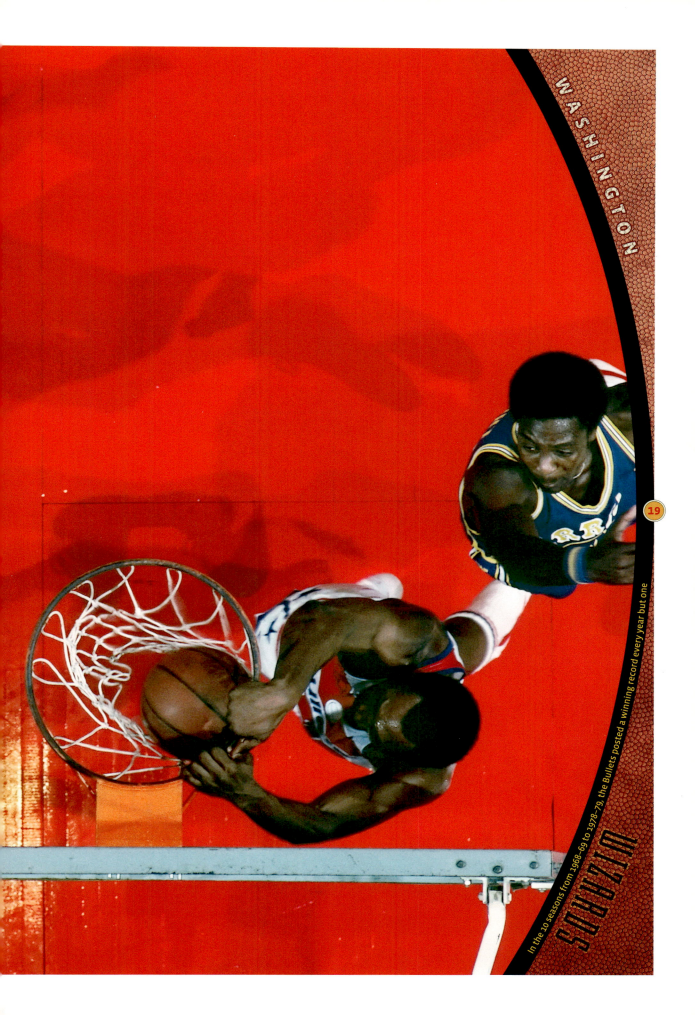

WIZARDS

In the 10 seasons from 1968-69 to 1978-79, the Bullets posted a winning record every year but one

19

THE MEDIOCRE YEARS

THE BULLETS NEARLY REPEATED AS CHAMPS THE

next season, but the SuperSonics got revenge by beat-

ing Washington in the NBA Finals. As it turned out, that

was the mighty Bullets' last run. In 1980, Coach Motta

left town, and a year later, Unseld retired and Hayes was

traded. The Bullets tried rebuilding around the "Bruise

Brothers" combination of tough center Jeff Ruland and

forward Rick Mahorn but fell into a slump.

Fans saw a number of talented players wear Bullets jer-

seys in the 1980s. Among them were Gus Williams, an

acrobatic point guard nicknamed "The Wizard"; Manute

Bol, a 7-foot-7 shot-blocking sensation; Jeff Malone,

a versatile guard with a great shooting touch; and

21

WIZARDS

Skyscraping center Manute Bol loved to shoot from long-distance, launching 91 "threes" in 1988–89

22

Hall of Fame forward Bernard King scored almost 20,000 career points, including 60 in a single game

high-scoring forward Bernard King. In 1988, the team even brought back star Wes Unseld as its new head coach. Yet despite all efforts, the Bullets were a painfully average team throughout the decade, finishing between 31–51 and 43–39 every season.

The 1990s started out even worse. In fact, it wasn't until 1994 that things began looking up in Washington. That season, Jim Lynam replaced Unseld as head coach. The bigger story, though, was the Bullets' new forward duo of Juwan Howard and Chris Webber. Howard arrived first via the 1994 NBA Draft. Then, early in the 1994–95 season, Washington added Webber in a trade with the Golden State Warriors.

Howard and Webber had been college teammates at the University of Michigan—two-fifths of the Wolverines' famous "Fab Five" lineup—and their reunion in Washington gave Bullets fans hope. While Howard was known for his steadiness and smart play, Webber gave the team strength and a deft passing touch. With these players lined up next to Gheorghe Muresan, a 7-foot-7 center from Romania, the Bullets once again had one of the most impressive frontcourts in the NBA.

To get a player who could distribute the ball to these young stars and shooters such as Tracy Murray, the Bullets traded for point guard Rod Strickland, one of the NBA's top assists men. In 1996–97, Strickland helped the Bullets make the playoffs for the first time in 10 years. "[We] have a lot of young, athletic, talented big people," said Coach Lynam, "and to plant an experienced guard like Rod with them, I think that is a huge plus."

BOL THE BLOCKER

In 1985, the NBA welcomed its tallest player ever: 7-foot-7 center Manute Bol. When he was drafted by the Bullets that year, many people thought it was a publicity stunt. The African tribesman from Sudan spoke little English and was so skinny (barely 200 pounds) he looked almost cartoonish. It was not a stunt, though. Bol, who was said to have "the longest arms in the world" and could dunk standing flat-footed, led the NBA with 397 blocks during the 1985–86 season. The shot-blocking specialist, who would play 10 seasons in the NBA and become something of a league-wide fan favorite, had actually started his athletic career in a different sport. As Bol recalled, "People were telling me, you know you're too tall to play soccer, you should play basketball."

25

Well-traveled guard Rod Strickland played for nine different teams over the course of his NBA career

WIZARDS

NEW NAME, NEW CENTURY

4

IN 1997, THE BULLETS CHANGED THEIR NAME TO
the Wizards and moved into the brand-new MCI Center
in downtown Washington. A year later, hoping to replace
inconsistent youth with steady leadership, they traded
Webber for veteran guard Mitch Richmond. The trade
did little to help. Even though Richmond put on some
fine shooting performances, the Wizards remained a
mediocre team.

WIZARDS

2

One of the finest pure scorers of the '90s, Mitch Richmond netted almost 20 points a game in 1998-99

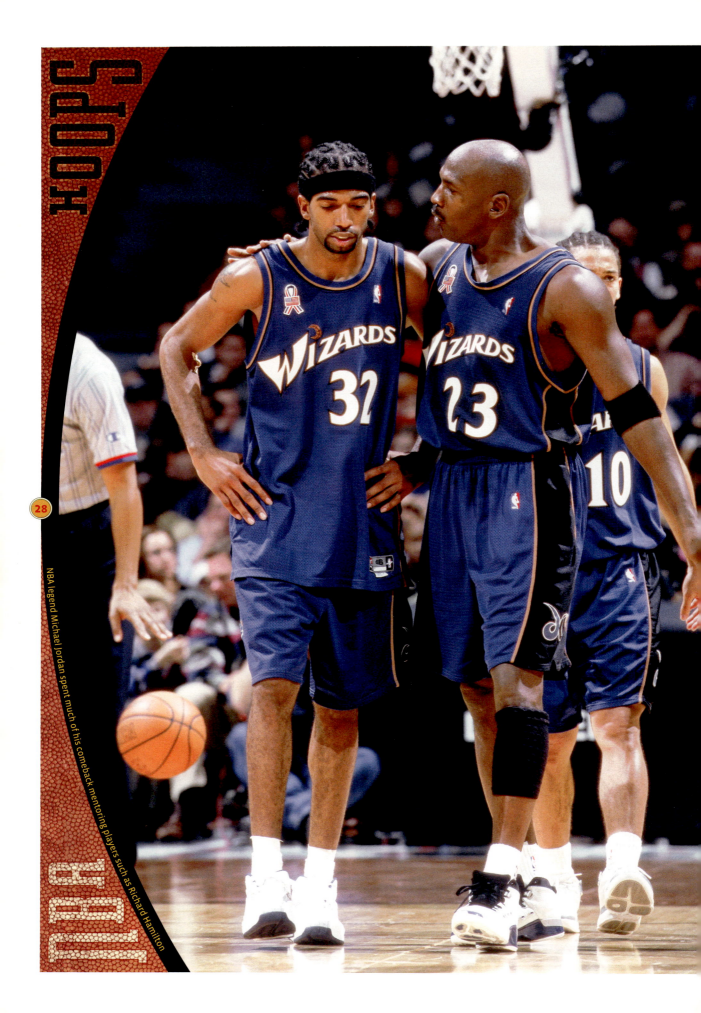

NBA legend Michael Jordan spent much of his comeback mentoring players such as Richard Hamilton

In 2000, a new star came to Washington: Michael Jordan, a former NBA guard who had led the Chicago Bulls to six world championships in the 1990s. At first, Jordan joined the Wizards as part owner and president of basketball operations. But in 2001, he pulled on a Wizards jersey and returned to action alongside young guard Richard Hamilton. His "unretirement" made major headlines, and he proved he had something left by scoring 40 points in a game a few days after turning 40 years old in 2002. But even Jordan could not make the Wizards big winners.

Jordan retired from the NBA for good after two seasons and left the Washington spotlight to new standouts such as forward Antawn Jamison and guard Gilbert Arenas. In 2004–05, the Wizards' new lineup gave fans reason for optimism by going 45–37 and making the playoffs. Arenas emerged as an All-Star, averaging more than 25 points per game, while Jamison led the team's inside attack. "We have great team chemistry," said Jamison. "This is just the start of something that we're going to make last for a long time."

Since its formation in 1961, the Wizards franchise has played under four different names in three different cities. But throughout those changes, the organization's commitment to winning has never faltered, resulting in one NBA championship and a parade of stars from Wes Unseld to Michael Jordan. Today's Wizards fans hope that this commitment will soon make Washington the capital of the basketball world once again.

WHAT'S IN A NAME?

The Wizards franchise was born as the Chicago Packers, a reference to Chicago's meat-packing history. Then, in its second year, it was renamed the Zephyrs, after the Greek god of the west wind (appropriate, since Chicago is nicknamed the "Windy City"). Upon moving to Baltimore in 1963, the team became known as the Bullets in honor of another NBA franchise that had played in Baltimore in the 1940s and '50s (that franchise had received the "Bullets" name because it played its home games in an armory, or weapons storage building). The final name change, in 1997, was made because many people found the name "Bullets" too violent. After fans sent in suggestions, "Wizards" was selected as the new name over such other possibilities as Monuments, Express, and Seadogs.

WIZARDS

Antawn Jamison was a versatile star whose resume included a 51-point game and a 21-rebound game

A

Arenas, Gilbert 29

B

Baltimore Bullets 10, 12, 15

Baltimore, Maryland 10, 12, 15

Basketball Hall of Fame 10

Bellamy, Walt ("Bells") 10, **10**

Bol, Manute 20, **21**, 24, **24**

"Bruise Brothers" 20

C

Capital Centre 15

Chenier, Phil 15

Chicago, Illinois 8

Chicago Packers 8, 10, 30

Chicago Zephyrs 8, 30

D

Dandridge, Bob 16

Dischinger, Terry 10

H

Hamilton, Richard **28**, 29

Hayes, Elvin ("The Big E") **14**, 15, 16, 20

Howard, Juwan 23

J

Jamison, Antawn 29, **30–31**

Johnson, Gus 5, 12

Jordan, Michael **28**, 29

K

King, Bernard 16, **16**, **22**, 23

L

Leonard, Bob 10

Loughery, Kevin 5

Lynam, Jim 23

M

Mahorn, Rick 20

Malone, Jeff 20

MCI Center 26

Monroe, Earl ("The Pearl") 5, 10, **11**, 12, 15

Most Valuable Player Award 12

Motta, Dick 16, 20

Muresan, Gheorghe 23

Murray, Tracy 23

N

NBA championship 16, 29

NBA Finals 15, 16, 20

NBA playoffs 10, 15, 16, 20, 23, 29

O

Ohl, Don 10

P

Porter, Kevin **17**

R

Richmond, Mitch 26, **27**

Ruland, Jeff 20

S

Scott, Ray 12

Shue, Gene 10

Strickland, Rod 23, **24–25**

U

Unseld, Wes 5, 12, **13**, 15, 16, 20, 23, 29

W

Washington Bullets 15, 16, 20, 23, 30

Washington Wizards

first season 8, 10

name 26, 30

relocations 8, 10

team records 15

Webber, Chris 23, 26

Williams, Gus ("The Wizard") 20